First World War
and Army of Occupation
War Diary
France, Belgium and Germany

39 DIVISION
Divisional Troops
Sherwood Foresters (Nottinghamshire and Derbyshire Regiment)
1/7th Battalion
1 August 1918 - 7 June 1919

WO95/2577/3

The Naval & Military Press Ltd
www.nmarchive.com
Published in association with The National Archives

Published by

The Naval & Military Press Ltd

Unit 10 Ridgewood Industrial Park,

Uckfield, East Sussex,

TN22 5QE England

Tel: +44 (0) 1825 749494

www.naval-military-press.com

www.nmarchive.com

This diary has been reprinted in facsimile from the original. Any imperfections are inevitably reproduced and the quality may fall short of modern type and cartographic standards.

© **Crown Copyright**
Images reproduced by permission of The National Archives, London, England, 2015.

Contents

Document type	Place/Title	Date From	Date To
Heading	WO95/2577/3		
Heading	39th Division 7th Bn Sherwood Foresters 1918 Aug-1919 Jun From 59 Dn. 178 Bde		
War Diary	Abancourt	01/08/1918	14/08/1918
War Diary	Blargies	15/08/1918	15/08/1918
War Diary	Calais	16/08/1918	16/08/1918
War Diary	Beaumarais	21/08/1918	31/08/1918
Miscellaneous	D.A.G., 3rd Echelon Base.	18/10/1918	18/10/1918
Miscellaneous	War Diary 7th (Robin Hood) Batt'n Sherwood Foresters September 1918		
War Diary	Beaumarais Near Calais	01/09/1918	05/09/1918
Miscellaneous	War Diary 7th (Robin Hood) Bn. Sherwood Foresters October. 1918		
War Diary	Calais	01/10/1918	29/10/1918
War Diary	Beaumarais Near Calais	01/11/1918	23/11/1918
Heading	War Diary Of The 7th. (Robin Hood) Bn. Sherwood Foresters. December 1918 Volume 46		
War Diary	Calais	01/12/1918	13/12/1918
War Diary	Havre	14/12/1918	31/12/1918
Miscellaneous	War Diary of 7th. (Robin Hood) Bn. The Sher. Foresters. For Month Of August 1918 Volume 43		
Miscellaneous	War Diary 7th (Robin Hood) Bn. Sherwood Foresters Month Of January 1919 Volume 47		
War Diary	Le Havre	01/01/1919	27/01/1919
Miscellaneous	Appendix "A"	01/09/1918	01/09/1918
Heading	War Diary Of For February 1919 Vol 48		
War Diary	Sanvic (Le Havre)	01/02/1919	26/02/1919
War Diary	Le Havre	01/02/1919	20/02/1919
War Diary	Sanvic (Le Havre)	01/04/1919	01/05/1919
Miscellaneous	War Diary Of 7th (Robin Hood) Bn Sherwood Foresters Vol No. 51 May 1919		
War Diary	No 1 Dispatch Camp Le Havre	01/05/1919	31/05/1919
Miscellaneous	On His Majesty's Service.		
War Diary	Wargnies-Le-Petit	01/06/1919	19/06/1919
War Diary	Cambai	20/06/1919	20/06/1919
War Diary	Boulogne	21/06/1919	24/06/1919
War Diary		04/06/1919	07/06/1919

W095/25471/3

39TH DIVISION

7TH BN SHERWOOD FORESTERS

~~AUG-DEC 1918~~

1918 AUG — 1919 JUN

From 59 DN, 178 BDE

7th Battn (Robin Hoods) Sherwood Foresters

Army Form C. 2118.

WAR DIARY
or
INTELLIGENCE SUMMARY.

August.

(Erase heading not required.)

Place	Date	Hour	Summary of Events and Information	Remarks and references to Appendices
ABANCOURT	1/8/18 to 14/8/18	9-12	Training carried on in Lewis Gun, Gas, Musketry and Bayonet fighting. Afternoons were devoted to Sports. During this period the Bn attn was attached to the 198 Bde of the 66th Division.	NIL
BLARGIES	15/8/18	10 pm	Battn came under the orders of the 39th Division and marched to BLARGIES station arriving there at 10 pm, and entrained with the 4th East Lancs Regt and proceeded to CALAIS	NIL
CALAIS	16/8/18	1 pm	The Battn arrived at CALAIS & proceeded to No 1 Canadian Camp BEAUMARAIS	NIL
BEAUMARAIS	21/8/18	4 pm	The Battn moved to the Officers Training Depot, with the 4th East Lancs Regt. The two Bn attns formed one group under the command of Colonel Norton D.S.O of the 4th East Lancs Regt.	NIL
BEAUMARAIS	21/8/18 & 31/8/18	8-12 & 2-4	The Battn formed working parties for the R.E.s and assisted them in building the Officers Training Camp.	NIL

19

SECRET AND CONFIDENTIAL.

HEADQUARTERS.
A.A. & Q.M.G.,
39TH DIVISION.
39/113/A

D.A.G.,
   3rd Echelon,
      Base.

    Reference 39/113/A dated 16.10.1918.

    Herewith War Diary for 7th (Robin Hood) Battalion, Sherwood Foresters, for month of September, 1918.

18th October, 1918.

                      Major-General,
            Commanding, 39th Division.

WAR DIARY.

7th (Robin Hood) Batt'n Sherwood Foresters.

September 1918.

Army Form C. 2118.

WAR DIARY
INTELLIGENCE SUMMARY

7th Bn. The Sherwood Foresters
September 1918

(Erase heading not required.)

Instructions regarding War Diaries and Intelligence Summaries are contained in F.S. Regs., Part II. and the Staff Manual respectively. Title pages will be prepared in manuscript.

Place	Date	Hour	Summary of Events and Information	Remarks and references to Appendices
BEAUMARAIS near CALAIS	1st		During the whole month of September 1918, the 7th Bn. The Sherwood Foresters was ~~employed~~ attached to No. 4 Officers Training School, CALAIS, and employed on instructional duties, and in the building of the School Camp. A hundred Subaltern officers from the Infantry Base Depots in Calais usually attended the school daily, and were instructed in Physical and Bayonet Training, Games, Tactical Schemes and Lectures, and Interior Economy.	W.T.
	5th		2/Lieut T. WILLIAMSON was struck off the strength on proceeding to "K" Inf. B.T. Base Depot.	B.T.
			2/Lieut L.K. BEARD was taken on the strength from "K" Inf. Base Depot	

W. Foster Capt & Adjt
for Lieut.-Col. Cdg.

CONFIDENTIAL.

WAR DIARY.

7th (ROBIN HOOD) Bn. SHERWOOD FORESTERS.

OCTOBER. 1918.

Instructions regarding War Diaries and Intelligence Summaries are contained in F. S. Regs., Part II. and the Staff Manual respectively. Title pages will be prepared in manuscript.

WAR DIARY of 7th (Robin Hood) Batta, Army Form C. 2118.
or
INTELLIGENCE SUMMARY.

The Sherwood Foresters

October 1918

(Erase heading not required.)

Place	Date	Hour	Summary of Events and Information	Remarks and references to Appendices
CALAIS	1st Oct – 31st Oct		The 7th Sherwood Foresters remained at No 4. Officer Camp, Calais. During this period the construction of the camp was continued, and Officers came daily from the Infantry Base Depots for instruction in Tactical Exercises, Ponce. B.T. etc. A series of educational lectures were started in the district, which many Officers attended	W.T.
do	13th Oct		Capt D. J. Wuincott was struck off the Strength on reporting to Inspiration School Aldershot	W.T.
do	18th Oct		The Mayor and Sheriff of Nottingham, accompanied by Major A. W. Lee, D.S.O., visited the Battalion. The Mayor inspected the Battalion, and gave a short address to the Officers and Men.	W.T.
do	20th Oct		Lt. Col. R. B. Richmond, 7th Sherwood Foresters, assumed command of No 4 Officer camp, vice Lt. Col. G. T. Hortin D.S.O. He relinquished command on 29th Oct, on the arrival of Lt. Col. K. W. Sworny D.S.O.	W.T.
do	29th Oct			H.S.T.

R.B. Buchanan. Lieut- Colonel
Cmg. 7th (Robin Hood) Bn., Sherwood Foresters

Army Form C. 2118.

7th Bn (Robin Hood) Bn., The Sherwood Foresters November 1918

WAR DIARY
INTELLIGENCE SUMMARY
(Erase heading not required.)

Instructions regarding War Diaries and Intelligence Summaries are contained in F. S. Regs., Part II. and the Staff Manual respectively. Title pages will be prepared in manuscript.

7 Notts Derby Vol 22

Place	Date	Hour	Summary of Events and Information	Remarks and references to Appendices
BEAUMARAIS near CALAIS	November/18 1		The Battalion Cadre remained at No. 4 Officers' Camp, BEAUMARAIS the whole month, up till the closing of the School, daily Instruction was given to the Subaltern Officers of the Base Depôts, as had been done in September and October. The subjects dealt with included Bayonet Fighting, Recreational Training and Games, Tactical Schemes, Company Work, Map Reading, and Cookery.	W.T
"	15		2/Lt. L.R. BEARD proceeded to join No. 3 Young Soldiers Bn., and was struck off the strength.	W.T
"	19		2/Lt. W.L. HUDSON was struck off the strength on proceeding to England, sick.	W.T
"	21		The School was closed by order of G.H.Q. The Battalion Cadre remained in the School at BEAUMARAIS, and joined "A" Cadre Group, 39th Division with the 4th Bn. E. Lancashire Regt. Recreational Training, Route Marching, Physical and Bayonet Training were carried out in	W.T H6.T

Army Form C. 2118.

Page 2

WAR DIARY
or
INTELLIGENCE SUMMARY.
(Erase heading not required.)

Place	Date	Hour	Summary of Events and Information	Remarks and references to Appendices
	23		the mornings, and games were played in the afternoon.	W.T
			Captain D.J. WINNICOTT, M.C. rejoined the Battalion from the Senior Officers' School, ALDERSHOT, and was taken on the strength	W.T

R.B. Rickman
Lieut- Colonel,
7th (Robin Hood) Bn.
The Sherwood Foresters

27

| 7TH |
| (ROBIN HOOD) BATTN., |
| THE |
| SHERWOOD FORESTERS. |
| No. |
| Date |

C O N F I D E N T I A L.

WAR   DIARY

of the

7th. (ROBIN HOOD) BN. SHERWOOD FORESTERS.

DECEMBER   1918.

VOLUME 46.

DECEMBER 1st 1916

Army Form C.2118

7th "Robin Hood" Bn.
Sherwood Forester.

WAR DIARY
INTELLIGENCE SUMMARY

(Erase heading not required.)

Instructions regarding War Diaries and Intelligence Summaries are contained in F.S. Regs., Part II. and the Staff Manual respectively. Title pages will be prepared in manuscript.

Place	Date	Hour	Summary of Events and Information	Remarks and references to Appendices
CALAIS	1		Usual training of trench coy. at rest.	
	2		do	
	3		do	
	4		do	
	5		do	
	6		do	
	7		do	
	8		do	
	9		do	
	10		Entrained for Havre at 3 PM at FONTINETTES Station CALAIS	
	11		In train en route for Havre	
	12		do	
HAVRE	14		Detrained at GARE MARITIME - HAVRE and marched to No 2 Rest Camp.	
	16		Sent some drafts of candidates for commission to No 16 Lieutenant Section B. from GARE MARITIME	
			do	

DECEMBER 1915.   No 2.

7th Robin Hood (1/7th) Army Form C. 2118.
Sherwood Foresters

WAR DIARY
or
INTELLIGENCE SUMMARY.
(Erase heading not required.)

Instructions regarding War Diaries and Intelligence
Summaries are contained in F. S. Regs., Part II.
and the Staff Manual respectively. Title pages
will be prepared in manuscript.

Place	Date	Hour	Summary of Events and Information	Remarks and references to Appendices
HAVRE	17.		Draft landing from Shoreham to No 1 Rest Camp Sent 13	
"	18.		do	
"	19.		do	
"	20.		do	
"	21.		do	
"	22.		do	
"	23.		Same moved from No 2 Rest together to No 1 Rest Camp.	
"			Section B. Sent over No 1 Rest Camp + help men to	
"			own own Z Section demobilisation for Rouen, Shoreliffe, Dagon	
"	24.		were hoped for demobilisation for Rouen, Shoreliffe, Dagon	
"			+ Chelsea draftes at centre.	
"	25.		Same men dates of receiving draft arriving at Z camp.	
"	26.		do	
"	27.		do	
"	28.		do	
"	29.		do	
"	30.		do	
"	31.		do	

N.B. Lt/Col J.mm Heatcote
(Comdg 7th (Robin Hood) Bn Sherwood Foresters

CONFIDENTIAL.

WAR DIARY
of
7th. (Robin Hood) Bn. The Sher. Foresters,
for month of August 1918.

VOLUME 43.

War Diary

4/3   39

7th (Robin Hood) Bn. Sherwood Foresters

Month of January

1919

Volume 47.

7TH
(ROBIN HOOD) BATTN.,
THE
SHERWOOD FORESTERS

B1393
5·2·19

Army Form C. 2118.

7th (Robin Hood) Battalion Sherwood Foresters WAR DIARY for January 1919

INTELLIGENCE SUMMARY.

(Erase heading not required.)

Instructions regarding War Diaries and Intelligence Summaries are contained in F. S. Regs., Part II. and the Staff Manual respectively. Title pages will be prepared in manuscript.

Place	Date	Hour	Summary of Events and Information	Remarks and references to Appendices
LE HAVRE	Jan/19		During the whole month the Battalion Cadre was employed in running the Concentration Camp for LE HAVRE Base at SANVIC, LE HAVRE. All men from the HAVRE area were received at the Camp, organised into parties for the various dispersal stations in England, and sent on to their appropriate Embarkation Camps. For this purpose the Cadre was organised in two "wings", each consisting of one Officer, one Warrant Officer, and two Sergeants, these "wings" worked in relief of each other, each wing being on duty for a stretch of 24 hours.	W.T.
	17th		A/Capt. R. B. GAMBLE proceeded to England for Demobilization; 4 other ranks was also demobilized.	W.T.
	27th		3 other ranks were demobilized.	W.T.

New Year Honours.

Mentioned in Despatches

Capt (A/Lt-Col) R. B. RICKMAN 5th (attd 7th) Sherwood Foresters
2nd Lieut W. L. HUDSON 7th Sherwood Foresters.

H.S.T.
7th West

[signature]
Capt. 7th Sherwood Foresters

APPENDIX 'A'.

Total Strength of Training Cadre 1-8-18.   9.   50.

    With Battn.   7.   47.
    Leave.   2.
    Attd. 1st. Wilts.   1.
    H.Q. Abancourt Area.   1.   -
    Signal School
    III Corps.   1.   -
                                   9.   50.   9.   50.

Total Strength 1-8-18.   9.   50.
    Increase.
      Reinforcement.   1.
      Trans. from
      6th. Bn. Lancs. Fus. 1. -   1.   1.
                                                          10.   51.

    Decrease.
      Trans. to 1st. Wilts. 1.
      In hosp. over 7
      days.   4.
      Proceeded to M.G.
      Centre, Grantham.   1.   -   1.   5.
                                                           9.   46.

Total Strength of Training Cadre 31-8-18.   9.   46.

    With Battn.   5.   39.
    Leave.   4.   5.
    In Hospital.   2.
                                   9.   46.   9.   46.

In the field.   .... Captain.
  1-9-18.   Comdg. 7th. (Robin Hood) Bn. The Sherwood Foresters.

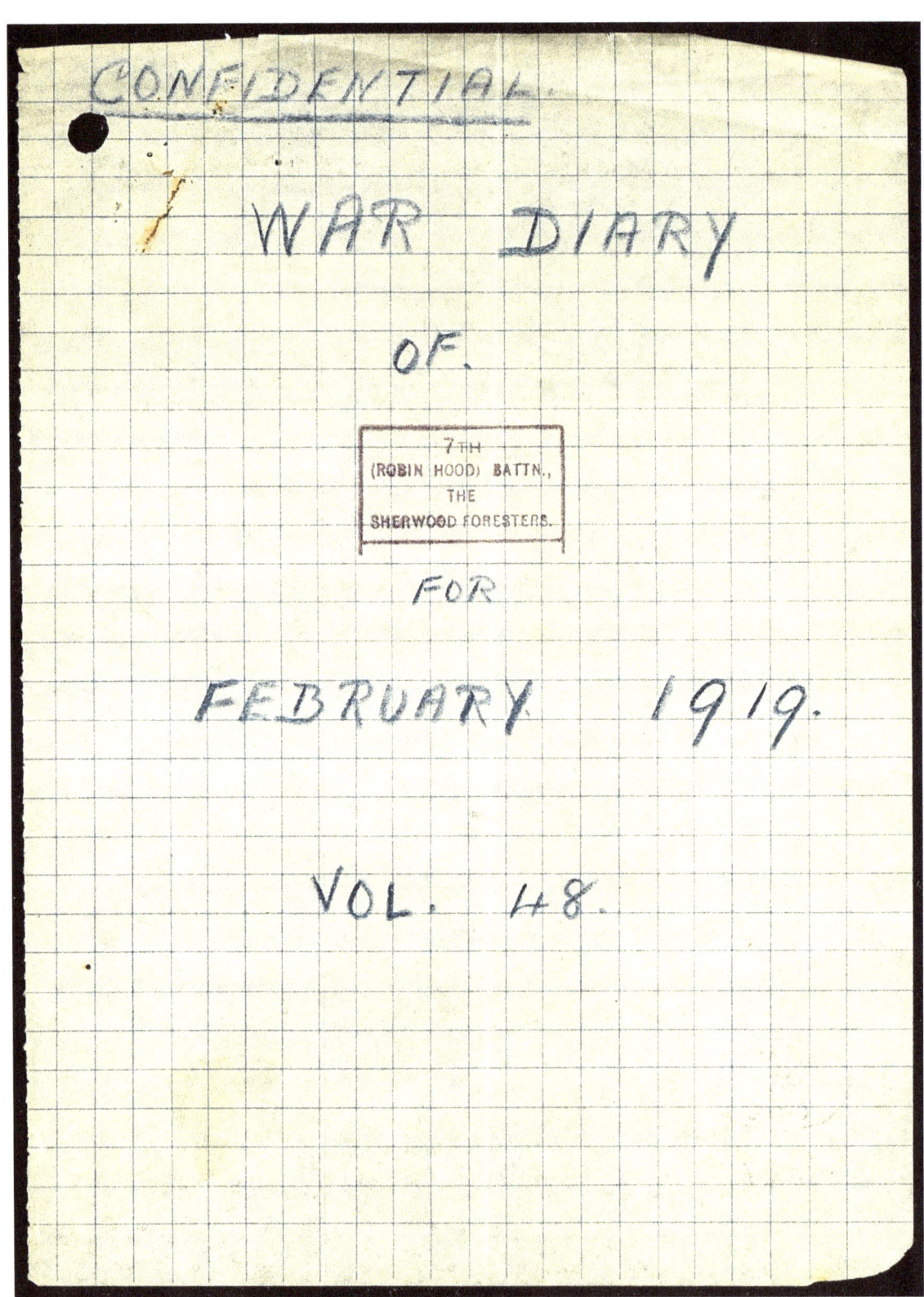

Army Form C. 2118.

WAR DIARY or INTELLIGENCE SUMMARY

1st/4th (Robin Hood) Bn. The Sherwood Foresters for **February 1919**

(Erase heading not required.)

Instructions regarding War Diaries and Intelligence Summaries are contained in F.S. Regs., Part II. and the Staff Manual respectively. Title pages will be prepared in manuscript.

Place	Date	Hour	Summary of Events and Information	Remarks and references to Appendices
SAULTAIN (LE BAURE)	1		The Battalion ensure continued to administer No 1 Concentration Camp SAULTAIN LE BAURE	
	2		The following officers were attached to the Battalion for duty: Lieut A.D.L. CHADBOURN 10th Lancers Regt 2/Lieut R.E. STARKEY 13th " " " R EVANS " " " L.H. SIZER 8th The Sherwood Foresters	
	25		11 Battalion orders handed over administration of Concentration Camps to Camp Staff under Major W.H. ZINCH R.G.A. and moved to No 1 Evacuation Camp SAULTAIN. At this Camp troops from the Corps are received from the Belgian Corps, inspected, shown to the train after a stay of 24 to 48 hours to consume there former and there own kits, suitable packed. The Battalion jointly with 7/7 Bn Northumberland Fusiliers administers To any dealing with men for Eastern and the North of England. Lieut CHADBOURN and 2/Lt EVANS detached for duty to Concentration Camp.	
	26		2/Lt R.E. STARKEY proceeded to join 4th Bn from R.	

R.B. Pickman Lieut-Col
Cmg. 1st/4th (R.H.) Bn The Sherwood Foresters

7th (Robin Hood) Bn. The Sherwood Foresters. WAR DIARY

Army Form C. 2118.

INTELLIGENCE SUMMARY /or March 1919

Place	Date	Hour	Summary of Events and Information	Remarks and references to Appendices
LE HAVRE	1		The Battalion Cadre continued throughout the month at No.1 Despatching Camp, SANVIC, LE HAVRE. Duties as before, consisted in receiving troops from the East and despatching them to the boat.	W.T.
	19		3 other ranks demobilized	W.T.
	20		6 other ranks reinforcements received	W.T.
			Strength on 1st March 6 officers 27 other ranks	W.T.
			" " 31st 6 " 30 " "	

W. Foster
Capt & Adjt
for O.C. 7th (R.H.) Bn.
The Sherwood Foresters

7th (Actv Hovt) Bn. the Sherwood Foresters

WAR DIARY for April 1919

Army Form C. 2118.

INTELLIGENCE SUMMARY.
(Erase heading not required.)

Place	Date	Hour	Summary of Events and Information	Remarks and references to Appendices
SANVIC (LE HAVRE)	April/19 1st		The Battalion Training Cadre remained at No.1 Departing Camp, SANVIC LE HAVRE, and continued to be employed in the administration of "T" Wing. During the month the number of troops passing through the Camp for demobilization diminished to practically nothing.	W.T.
	13th		A/R.S.M. J. BERRY proceeded to COLOGNE to take over appointment of R.S.M. to 1/4th Bn. York and Lancaster Regt., and is struck off strength.	W.T.
	20th		Captain J.S.C. OATES, D.S.O., M.C., proceeded to England for demobilization and is struck off strength.	W.T.
	26th		The Battalion, together with the other Cadre Battn. at No.1 Despatching Camp, was relieved of all duties in connection with machinery of demobilization by 18th (Pioneer) Bn. Middlesex Regiment.	W.T.

7th Shw. Foresters   Sheet 2

Army Form C. 2118.

WAR DIARY
or
INTELLIGENCE SUMMARY.
(Erase heading not required.)

Place	Date	Hour	Summary of Events and Information	Remarks and references to Appendices
			The Battalion commenced at No.1 Dispersing Camp for the rest of the month, obviously forgotten.	
			During the month 1 O.R. proceeded to England for demobily return and was struck off strength.	
			Strength on 30/4/19. Officers 5 (including 1 attached from 4 E. Lanc R) Other Ranks 22	
Sannois 1.5.19			R.B. McKewan Lt-Colonel Commanding 7th/(Notts Herts) Bn. The Sherwood Foresters	

Confidential.

War Diary

of

7th (Robin Hood) Bn Sherwood Foresters

VOL. No. 51.

May. 1919

MAY 1919   5TH (ROBIN HOOD) 7TH   Army Form C. 2118.
   THE SHERWOOD FORESTERS

WAR DIARY
or
INTELLIGENCE SUMMARY.
(Erase heading not required.)

Instructions regarding War Diaries and Intelligence Summaries are contained in F. S. Regs., Part II and the Staff Manual respectively. Title pages will be prepared in manuscript.

Place	Date	Hour	Summary of Events and Information	Remarks and references to Appendices
No 1 DISPATCH CAMP	1st		Battalion resting in camp awaiting embarkation	J.6/28
LE HAVRE	19		" " " "	
do	"		Lt Col W Foster MC handed over to England for demobilization	
			awaiting demobilization	

Signed H. Collis Major
for Lt Col 7 Sherwood [Foresters]

ON HIS MAJESTY'S SERVICE.

Henry Want Esq
Messrs Scheew Roemers
War Office
Balfour House
Finsbury Pavement
London

Army Form C. 2118.

WAR DIARY
or
INTELLIGENCE SUMMARY.
(Erase heading not required.)

Place	Date	Hour	Summary of Events and Information	Remarks and references to Appendices
Harfleur Rest Camp	1st Mar. 1919		Church Parade. 6 ORs struck off strength.	
"	2nd		General fatigue duty.	
"	3rd		do	
"	4th		do	2 ORs rejoined from leave and 1 OR to hospital.
"	5th		do	
"	6th		do	
"	7th		do	2 ORs rejoined from leave. 1 OR proceeds to 151st Inf. Bde.
"	8th		do	2 ORs proceeded to Havre for dental treatment. 1 OR to hospital.
"	9th		do	
"	10th		do	
"	11th		do	
"	12th		do	4 ORs rejoined from leave
"	13th		do	
"	14th		Church Parade. Sunday fatigues. General fatigue duty.	
"	15th			
"	16th		Lieut A. Rhodes & (Army) Staff Officer who had arrived at Havre this day reported to Base H.Q. Havre but going on to C.H.B.S Deboirville, Hazebrouck to Quevey Boulogne	

53.T.
grown

7th Machine Gun Corps

Army Form C. 2118

WAR DIARY
or
INTELLIGENCE SUMMARY.
(Erase heading not required.)

Place	Date	Hour	Summary of Events and Information	Remarks and references to Appendices
Italy	21		Halted at Sturla for camp for one to press KOK	General note
	22		do	A214
	23		do	N214
	24		Coy. deft for a train disposal area	K214

WAR DIARY

7th Sherwood Foresters
June 1919

Month	Date	Summary	Ref.
June	4th	Orders received for disbandment of Division	S/Garres
June	4th	Stores, Vehicles & Harness handed in to A.O.D HAVRE	S/
June	5th	Horses proceeded by march Route to ROUEN and handed in to Remount Depôt	S/
June	6th	Farewell order received from G.O.C. 39th Division, copy attached.	S/
June	7th	Cadre proceeded to No 2 Reception Camp, HARFLEUR HAVRE for demobilization	S/

www.ingramcontent.com/pod-product-compliance
Lightning Source LLC
Chambersburg PA
CBHW081250170426
43191CB00037B/2103

Sheet 29 —1—   Secret.
         40,000.
                                 Copy No.
Operation Order No 19 by Captain
R.D. Flunder, Com. 1/7 Wks Reg.

                              24.10.18
Para 1. 1/7 Wks Bns will clear WOOD in
   ✓ 18 c + d & village of BOSSUYT
   ✓ 13 c + d.
   2. The artillery programme is as
      follows. At Z hour for two
      minutes will bombard line —
      edge of wood from U 18 c. 0.5 to
      ✓ 7 c. 8.2. The barrage will lift
      100 yards each 3 minutes to a
      line from V 24 b 23 to V 13 d 9.4 where
      it will remain for half an hour.
Para 3. Two sections R.E. with rafts
      & a carrying party of pioneers
      (Somerset L.I.) will be in readiness
      to place rafts in position on canal
      when bridge-heads have been
      established by attacking companies.
Para 4. D. Coy will attack along line
      of canal between LOCKS 3 & 5
      both inclusive, and
      will establish bridge-heads
      sending back to forward R.E.
      dump for rafts to cross
      immediately. The
      Company will cross canal &

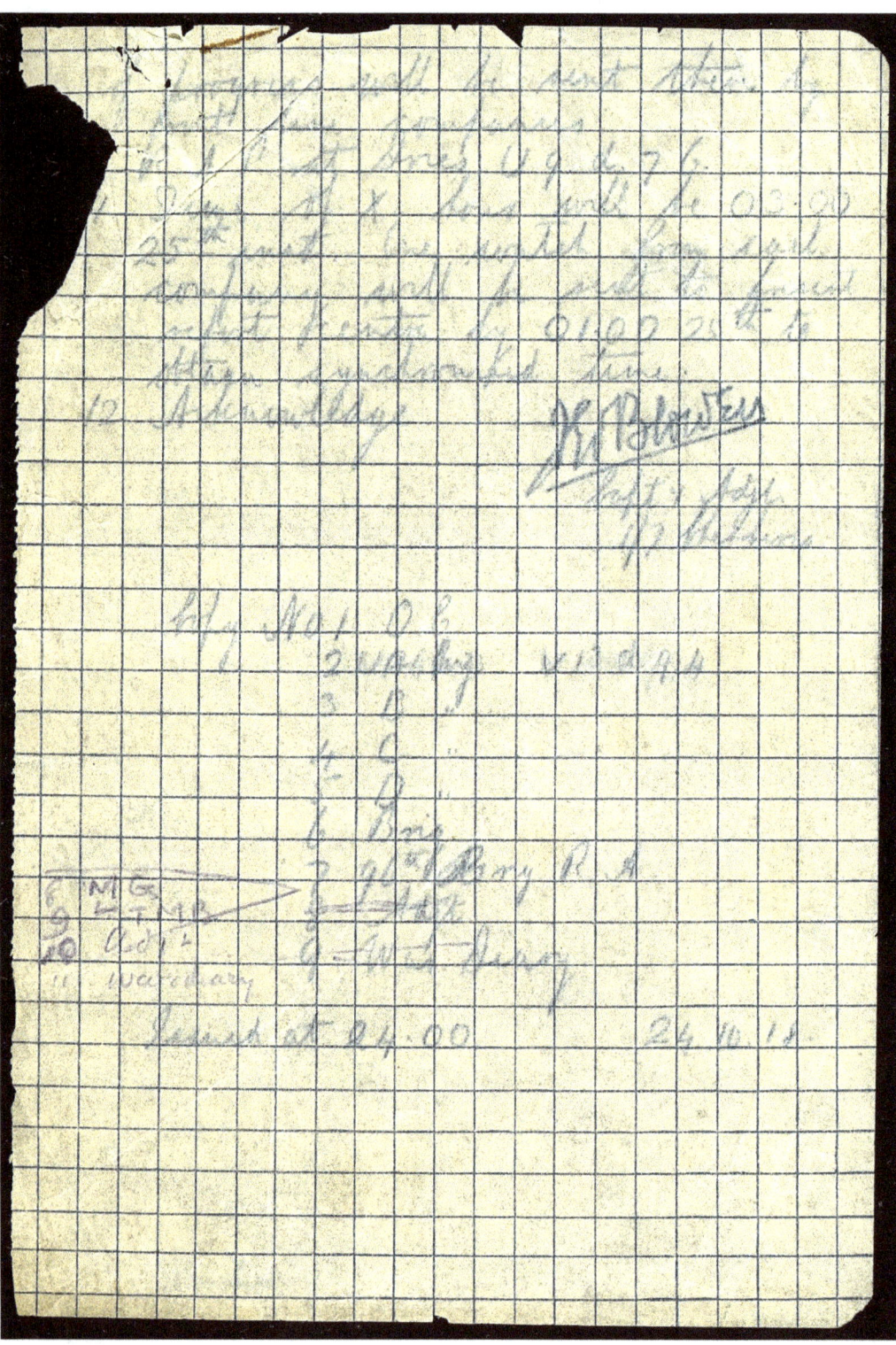

establish a line along the road
from U12 f.9.8. S.E. to BOSSUYT.
Position of H.Q. during will be
notified later.
Para 5. A Coy on right & D. Coy on
left will follow barrage closely
through WOOD to RIVER
SCHELDT & establish line along
northern bank from U 24 b on right
to V 13 a.5.7. on left, C Coy.
clearing up village of BOSSUYT.
6. B Coy will be in Reserve & will
move at X hour to positions
vacated by A. Coy.
7. M Gy & L.T.M. O's attached to
battalion carry out a programme
to be issued separately.
8. The 41st DIV. & 4 CORPS are
attacking east of canal in a
S.E. direction at 09.00 2.5th inst.
As soon as the attacking lines
pass our front line positions
of D Coy OC D. Coy will swing
his left flank round to
support attack & reinforce line
if necessary.
9. Signal Officer will run a line
from Batt forward report centre
to MOELDRIESCH U 12 C.0.0.
before X hour & with reports to

Also my Acting Adjutant Lieut G R MONTAGUE. I have already brought his fine bold work through MENIN on 14th October, he being the first to enter the town. Although he only took over the duties of Acting Adjutant on the 20th he has been of the greatest assistance to me. He is clearheaded, decided & practical and under circumstances of great danger & difficulty keeps perfectly clear & calm. He accompanied me & together with 5 O runners & signallers the party proceeded through MOEN and reached U 6 d 3.6 well in advance of the rest of the Battalion.

Lieut & Q.M. ROTHWELL here as well as at MENIN managed the supply & arrangements for Battn Rations with great success. He personally superintended the above office under heavy M.G & Shell fire.

22.30.
27.10.18

Lt Col.
Officer Commanding 1/4th Cheshire Regt

Sheet 1.

WAR DIARY
or
INTELLIGENCE SUMMARY.
(Erase heading not required.)

Army Form C. 2118.

17TH BATTALION
1 DEC 1918
THE CHESHIRE REGT.

Place	Date	Hour	Summary of Events and Information	Remarks and references to Appendices
Sheet 29 1/40,000	1.XII.18		HARLEBEKE All Coys fired on Lewis gun range. Musketry training carried out on 30 Y range. 100 men fitted.	7.Y
	2.XII.18	15.30	E.A. dropped 4 bombs. One NCO wounded.	7.Y
	3.XII.18	07.30	Training carried on as for previous day. Enemy shelled HARLEBEKE with H.Vs. Bn. left HARLEBEKE at head of Brigade group, march to MOORSELE Route - LYS R. crossed at H.11.central - LEYHOEK - CUERNE - WATERMOLEN - road running WEST through G.24,23 d.a. to MOORSELE	7.Y
Sheet 28 1/40,000		11.30	Arrived MOORSELE Bn. H.Q. L.23.a.6.5. Men billeted	7.Y
	4.XII.18		Bn. rested in morning, games in afternoon. Training programme submitted to Bgy H2	7.Y
	5.XII.18		Interior training carried on owing to wet weather.	
	6.XII.18		Lt.H. Mair resumed command. Programme of training as submitted to 102nd Brigade carried out. Instruction in rapid moving of platoons given to A + D Coys	7.Y
	7.XII.18		Programme of training ordinary work on Lewis gun range, live rifle grenade work, B + C Coys carried out Rapid Loading of platoon carried out by B + C Coys	
	8.XII.18		Brigade sport proceeded to R.Coys and carried out construction of bridge + raft across river.	7.Y
	9.XII.18		A + D Coys inspected by C.O. Training Programme carried out.	7.Y
	10.XII.18	10.30	Brigade Church Parade at L.23.c.0.6.	7.Y
		21.00	Germans accepted terms of armistice.	7.Y
	11.XI.18	11.00	Armistice commenced. Day declared a holiday.	7.Y

Army Form C. 2118.

Sheet II

WAR DIARY
or
INTELLIGENCE SUMMARY.
(Erase heading not required.)

Instructions regarding War Diaries and Intelligence Summaries are contained in F.S. Regs., Part II. and the Staff Manual respectively. Title pages will be prepared in manuscript.

Place	Date	Hour	Summary of Events and Information	Remarks and references to Appendices
Sheet 28 / 40,000	12.XI.18	09.00	B + C Coys inspected by C.O. Programme of training carried out.	7.4
	13.XI.18		Bn. carried out programme of training, including practice in "Platoon Syst".	7.4
	14.XI.18		Brig. gp't moved to BELLEGHEM area. Bn. passed starting point Bdy N.2 MOORSEELE at 09.67. Route WELVEGHEM - LAUWE - AELBEKE - ROLLEGHEM - BELLEGHEM. Bn. billets Br. N.2. N 33 a 6.2.	7.4
		12.35	Bn. arrived BELLEGHEM.	7.4
Tournai Sheet 1 / 100,000	15.XI.18		Brig. gp't moved to CELLES. Starting point Sq.M. in BELLEGHEM. Bn. passed at 09.01. Route COYGHEM - road through A in GAVRE - HELGHIN BRIDGE - POTTES. Bn. billeted in CELLES.	7.4
	16.XI.18	14.00	Brig. gp't moved to RENAIX. Bn. passed starting point on main TOURNAI ROAD at 10.37. Route CELLES - ANSERAVT. Bn. arrived Renaix at 14.00.	7.4
17.XI.18		10.30	Church Parade.	7.4
	18.XI.18		Brig. gp't moved to FLOBECQ - WODECQ area. Starting pt. Railway crossing 500× E. of Renaix in RENAIX - ELLESELLE Rd. Route - Renaix - ELLESELLES - FLOBECQ RD. Bn. passed starting point at 09.13. Arrived FLOBECQ at 12.00.	7.4
	19.XI.18	09.00	Ceremonial parade. Training if sports in afternoon.	7.4
	20.XI.18		Ceremonial parade & close order drill. Sports in afternoon.	7.4
	21.XI.18	10.00	Bn. bus transport inspected by O.C. 6.102 Brigade.	7.4
	22.XI.18	09.00	Bn. paraded for route march to BOIS.	7.4
	23.XI.18	09.00	Physical training. Interior economy.	7.4

Sheet III

Army Form C. 2118.

WAR DIARY
or
INTELLIGENCE SUMMARY.
(Erase heading not required.)

Instructions regarding War Diaries and Intelligence Summaries are contained in F. S. Regs., Part II. and the Staff Manual respectively. Title pages will be prepared in manuscript.

Place	Date	Hour	Summary of Events and Information	Remarks and references to Appendices
Sept Sommaise Shot	24.XI.18	11.00	Brigade Church Parade.	7.Y
	25.XI.18	9.00	Training Programme carried out.	7.Y
	26.XI.18	9.00	Bn. paraded for training under C.O.	7.Y
	27.XI.18		Day devoted to interior economy + cleaning	7.Y
	28.XI.18	9.00	Bn. inspected by C.O.	7.Y
	29.XI.18	10.30	Brigade guard inspected by G.O.C. 34th Div.	7.Y
	30.XI.18	9.00	Physical Drill for one hour. Interior Economy + Cleaning Billets	7.Y
			Brigade Church Parade	

Signed H.L. Moir
Lt Col
Comdg 1/7th Batt. Cheshire Regt.

Army Form C. 2118.

Sheet I. 1/7 Cheshires

WAR DIARY
or
INTELLIGENCE SUMMARY

(Erase heading not required.)

Place	Date	Hour	Summary of Events and Information	Remarks and references to Appendices
Lessines 105,000	1.12.18	10.30	Brigade Church Parade. FLOBECQ.	7.4.
	2.12.18	0.900	Bn. route march to WODECQ.	7.4.
	3.12.18	0.900	Bn. drill under Commanding Officer. Working party 3 offs + 100 O.Rs. on LESSINES ROAD.	7.4.
	4.12.18	0.900	Bn. route march to BOIS.	7.4.
	5.12.18	0.900	Bn. drill under C.O. Three extra drill + ceremonial under company arrangements.	7.4.
	6.12.18	0.900	Training under company arrangements.	7.4.
	7.12.18	0.900	Bn. drill under C.O.	7.4.
	8.12.18	10.30	Brigade Church Parade.	7.4.
			Bn. route march – POITERIE – MOTTE – HURDMONT – FLOBECQ.	7.4.
	9.12.18	09.00	Bn. drill under C.O. Preliminary inspection for medal distribution of 400 O.Rs.	7.4.
	10.12.18	09.15	Bn. drill under C.O.	7.4.
	11.12.18	11.00	Distribution of medal ribbons by G.O.C. Division 20 offs & O.Rs.	7.4.
	12.12.18	0.900	Brigade route march to GHISLENGHIEN area. Bn. found starting point OGY.	7.4.
			Bn. at 10.00. Route OGY – LESSINES. Bn. billeted at HELLEBECQ.	7.4.
⅞	13.12.18	0.900	Bn. rested & cleaned up.	7.4.
	14.12.18	09.20	Bn. moved with Brigade Group to SOIGNIES area. Found starting point on LESSINES – SOIGNIES ROAD at 10.33. Route – HELLEBECQ – SILLY – SOIGNIES. Bn. billeted in SOIGNIES at 14.00.	7.4.
New Europe 210,000	15.12.18	08.00	Bn. rested. Voluntary church services held.	7.4.
	16.12.18	07.15	Brigade group moved to LAHESTRE area. Bn. found starting point HAUTE FOLIE cross roads at 08.33. Bn. billeted in HAIN ST. PAUL.	7.4.
	17.12.18	08.00	Brigade group moved to MARCHIENNE AU PONT. Arrived at MARCHIENNE at 6.0pm. Bn. billeted	7.4.

Sheet II

Army Form C. 2118.

WAR DIARY
or
INTELLIGENCE SUMMARY.
(Erase heading not required.)

Instructions regarding War Diaries and Intelligence Summaries are contained in F. S. Regs., Part II. and the Staff Manual respectively. Title pages will be prepared in manuscript.

Place	Date	Hour	Summary of Events and Information	Remarks and references to Appendices
NW Europe 1/250,000	18.12.18	09.40	Btn. continued its march to CHATELET. Rnte via MONCEAU SUR SAMBRE & BINCHE-CHARLEROI road. Arrived CHATELET at 13.00. Btn. billeted in BOUFFIOULX.	Him
	19.12.18	07.15	Btn. continued its march to FOSSE. Route via PRESLES-VITRIVAL FOSSES roads. Arrived FOSSE at 11.50. Btn. billetted.	Him
	20.12.18	09.00	Cleaning up & inspecting.	Him
	21.12.18	09.00	Cleaning up & inspecting.	Him
	22.12.18	09.30	Voluntary Church Service.	Him
	23.12.18	09.00	C.O. inspected billets. Infantry training under O.C. Companies.	Him
	24.12.18	09.00	Bn drill under C.O. - Coy drill under Coy Commander	Him
	25.12.18 26.12.18		Holidays -	Him
	27.12.18	09.00	Bn Route march - with transport to Aisemont and Vitrival Interior Economy - Inspection of Kits &c. C.O. inspection of Billets	Him
	28.12.18		Bde Church parade in Sqr opposite Hotel de Ville	Him
	29.12.18	10.00	Bn route march with transport. METTET ROAD - past ETAGE DE FOSSE and return along ST GERARD RD.	Him
	30.12.18	09.00		Him
	31.12.18	09.00	Inspection of Bn. in F.M.O. by C.O	Him

H. Knox
Lieut. Colonel
Cmdg. 1/7 Cheshire Regt.

Army Form C. 2118.

WAR DIARY
or
INTELLIGENCE SUMMARY.

Sheet II.

(Erase heading not required.)

Place	Date	Hour	Summary of Events and Information	Remarks and references to Appendices
Izel	8.1.19	08.50	Rifles of Btn. inspected by armourer. Boys had one hour training after rifle & after inspection	74
		14.30	Recreational training	
	9.1.19	09.30	Btn. paraded for route march accompanied by 1st line transport.	74
		14.30	Recreational training	
	10.1.19	09.45	Btn. including transport inspected by C.O.	74
		14.30	Recreational training	
	11.1.19		Morning devoted to interior economy, kit inspection & billet inspection under Coy arrangements.	74
		14.30	Btn. Cross country run of 3½ miles.	
	12.1.19	10.30	Voluntary C of E service in Hôtel de Ville. Newcomforts in Y.M.C.A.	74
	13.1.19	09.15	Btn. route march	74
		14.30	Recreational training	
	14.1.19	8.30	Btn. commenced batting by companies	74
		9.15	Btn. paraded as strong as possible for command drill under C.O.	
		14.30	Recreational training	

WAR DIARY or **INTELLIGENCE SUMMARY**

Army Form C. 2118.

(Erase heading not required.)

1/7 Cheshires Vol.

Place	Date	Hour	Summary of Events and Information	Remarks and references to Appendices
TOTAL	1.1.1919	09.30	Btn. paraded for B.F.O.D. & arms drill. Transport lines & vehicles inspected by Commanding Officer. Btn. billets inspected by C.O.	74
	2.1.1919	09.00	Btn. paraded for training in accordance with programme.	74
		11.00	Lecture by Capt. Dunn on "League of Nations". 30 O.R. attended. Blankets & clothing disinfected. Recreational training in afternoon	74
	3.1.1919	09.15	Btn. route march to Mont St. Laurent. Recreational training in afternoon.	74
	4.1.1919	09.00	Btn. paraded for training as per programme	74
		14.30	Recreational training	
	5.1.1919	09.00	Preparing for programme. Voluntary church services in Hôtel de Ville.	74
		14.30	Recreational training	
	6.1.1919	09.00	Btn. paraded for training as per programme	74
		14.30	Recreational training	
	7.1.1919	09.00	Btn. paraded for training as per programme	74
		11.00	be hour Btn. drill.	
		09.30	Billets inspected by C.O.	
		09.00	Lewis guns inspected by Armourer.	
		14.30	Recreational training	

Army Form C. 2118.

Sheet III

WAR DIARY
or
INTELLIGENCE SUMMARY.
(Erase heading not required.)

Instructions regarding War Diaries and Intelligence Summaries are contained in F. S. Regs., Part II. and the Staff Manual respectively. Title pages will be prepared in manuscript.

Place	Date	Hour	Summary of Events and Information	Remarks and references to Appendices
Fresnes	15.1.19	0.915	Bn. drill under A.O.	74
		14.30	Recreational Training.	74
	16.1.19	10.15	Bn. inspected by G.O.C. 102 Brigade	74
		14.30	Recreational training	74
	17.1.19	10.30	Brigade Drill & March past under G.O.C. 102 Brigade	74
		14.30	Recreational training.	74
	18.1.19	10.30	Medal distribution by G.O.C. 34th Division G.O.C. inspected Btn. Billets after distribution.	74
		14.30	Recreational training	74
	19.1.19	14.30	Voluntary Church Parade in Marcq in Villa.	74
		10.30	Lecture by 2nd i/c to N.C.Os. in Demobilization & reconstruction.	
		09.00	Recreational training	
		14.30		
	20.1.19	09.15	Bn. route march passing Ecurry de Torse.	74
		14.30	Recreational training	74
	21.1.19		Bn. cleaning up billets & preparing for move.	74
	22.1.19	11.00	Bn. relieved by 19th Canadian Infantry. Bn. marched to Auchois	74
		21.30	Bn. left Auchois	74

Army Form C. 2118.

WAR DIARY
or
INTELLIGENCE SUMMARY.
(Erase heading not required.)

Sheet IV

Instructions regarding War Diaries and Intelligence Summaries are contained in F. S. Regs., Part II. and the Staff Manual respectively. Title pages will be prepared in manuscript.

Place	Date	Hour	Summary of Events and Information	Remarks and references to Appendices
Beede	23.1.19	11.30	Btn. detained at Beede. Men billeted. A Coy. relieved by J & K Prussian Infantry in the outpost line.	74
	24.1.19		Cleaning up & adjusting billets. C.6. inspected billet area.	74
	25.1.19		C.6. inspected billet area.	74
	26.1.19	10.00	102 Bde Guard Parade in Church. Newyrimito [?] in G.H.Q. C.9. 2 Coy. formed holding piquet. C.O. visited outpost line with G.O.C. 102 Inf Brigade. Btn. not marched on. A. Halleby[?]	74
	27.1.19	09.00	Cleaning carried out, and company commanders educated, training & specialist work.	74
	28.1.19	09.00	Training as for 28th. Recreational training in afternoon.	74 74
	30.1.19		Btn. cleaning up & billets, preparing for move.	74
	31.1.19	09.30	Relief of Btn. completed by 15th H.L.I. of 15th Div. marched to Schnieur [?] via Shugbug [?] arriving at 13.15. Btn. billetted, and relief of 23rd Sredolisky [?] reported completed.	74

Lieut. Colonel
Cmdg. 1/7 Bn [?] [Battalion] Reserve.

WAR DIARY
or
INTELLIGENCE SUMMARY
(Erase heading not required.)

Army Form C. 2118.

Vol 9

Place	Date	Hour	Summary of Events and Information	Remarks and references to Appendices
	1/2/19		The Battalion of Gen. Mettle by C.O. & 2nd in Command.	
	2/2/19		One platoon of C. Coy. withdrawn from the ALTENRATH & billeted at Gr. ICHATHR. Bn. under Co. of Coy.	
	3/2/19		Coy. H.Q. established at LOHMAR. C Coy. move to ALTENRATH	
	4/2/19		All Coy. inspected by O.C. 1/14 of 6 Kentilies. Remarks by Bn. Comdg.	
			under Coy. arrangts.	
	5/2/19		See to Genl. instr. C.O. for General Drill lecture	
	6/2/19		A "C" Coy. attended lecture at ... HQ.M.	
	7/2/19	10.00	Bn. moved off under	
	8/2/19		leaving of dollies on leave to England & men.	
	9/2/19	11.00	Second Lecture for O.T.C Payot G. Capt L. Inspection	
	10/2/19	09.00	of men for present for Roll Check under S.O.	
	11/2/19	09.00	Bn. proceed under C.O. for General Drill.	
		11.15-12.15	Educational classes finished.	
	12/2/19	10.30-12.00	Educational classes finished & tenant training.	
	13/2/19	10.15	Bn. paraded under Capt. L. 13 in G. Guerville.	
			Bn. will remainder of 102 Inf. Bgde. inspected by	
			G.O.C. 34th Division, who thanked all ranks for	
	14/2/19		cleaning of rifles & bolts & working arrangt.	
	15/2/19		By S.O. Battn. inspected	

Sheet II

Army Form C. 2118.

WAR DIARY
or
INTELLIGENCE SUMMARY.
(Erase heading not required.)

Instructions regarding War Diaries and Intelligence Summaries are contained in F. S. Regs., Part II. and the Staff Manual respectively. Title pages will be prepared in manuscript.

Place	Date	Hour	Summary of Events and Information	Remarks and references to Appendices
Seraing	16/2/19	10.45	Church parade for C of E in Prison Chapel	Sgd.
	17/2/19	10.00	Boys carry out training under Coy arrangements.	Sgd.
	18/2/19	09.30 - 10.45	Coy training	Sgd.
		11.15 - 12.15	Educational & Specialist training	Sgd.
	19/2/19		Bn paraded for route march under 2nd in command.	Sgd.
	20/2/19	09.30 - 10.45	Coy training	Sgd.
		11.15 - 12.15	Educational & Specialist training	Sgd.
	21/2/19	09.30 - 11.30	Training under Coy arrangements	Sgd.
		11.00	Transport tested inspected by C.O.	Sgd.
	22/2/19	09.30	Inspection of Billets by C.O.	Sgd.
	23/2/19	10.00	Church parade for C of E in Prison Chapel	Sgd.
	24/2/19	09.30 - 12.00	Coy training including musketry exercises, guards drill.	Sgd.
	25/2/19	09.30 - 10.45	Training under Coy arrangements	Sgd.
		11.15 - 12.15	Educational Specialist training	Sgd.
	26/2/19		Baths allotted to Bn from 06.00 - 10.00	Sgd.
	27/2/19		Communication drill for all available offrs YNCOs & 60 O.Rs by C.R.E. Fatigue 20 O.Rs.) fatigue to Divn M.T. Coy.	Sgd.
		14.00	Warning order to move to Bercheim on 28.2.19 received.	Sgd.

(A7092) Wt. W12839/M1293. 75,000. 1/17. D.D. & L., Ltd. Forms/C.2118/14.

Sheet III

Army Form C. 2118.

WAR DIARY
or
INTELLIGENCE SUMMARY.
(Erase heading not required.)

Instructions regarding War Diaries and Intelligence Summaries are contained in F. S. Regs., Part II. and the Staff Manual respectively. Title pages will be prepared in manuscript.

Place	Date	Hour	Summary of Events and Information	Remarks and references to Appendices
SIEGBURG	26.2.19	09.30	Battn moved off from position on the march from SIEGBURG to BORNHEIM via BONN. Distance 13 miles.	
		15.30	Arrived at BORNHEIM & came under command of J.O.C. 1st Infantry Brigade, 1st Division. Bn H.Qrs, 'A' & 'B' Coys billeted in BORNHEIM, 'C' & 'D' Coys quartered in BRENIG.	Ay.

H. Moir,
Lieut-Colonel,
Commanding 1/7th Bn, The Cheshire Regt.

2.3.19

WAR DIARY
or
INTELLIGENCE SUMMARY.

Army Form C. 2118.

(Erase heading not required.)

Place	Date	Hour	Summary of Events and Information	Remarks and references to Appendices
Brocken	1/3/19		Coys devoted morning to settling into billets and interior economy.	
	2/3/19	0930	'A' & 'B' Coys paraded in Cinema for Divine Service.	
		1045	'C' & 'D' do do	
		1300	Batt. forms part of 1st Brigade, 1st Division	
			D Coy billet	
			Summer time came into force	
	3/3/19	0930	Batt. inspected by Commanding Officer	
			Batt. transport handed over in exchange for transport of 1st L.N.L.	
	4/3/19	0930	'C' & 'D' parades Coy training. 'A' Coy educational training	
	5/3/19	0930	Bn paraded for route march	
	6/3/19	0930	A,C,D Coy training, B Coy education	
	7/3/19	0930	A, B, Coy training, C, D, education	
	8/3/19	0930	Bn. Drill under Commanding Officer	
	9/3/19	1035	A & B parade for Divine Service	
		1015	C & D do	
	10/3/19	0930	A Coy move into billets vacated by 1st L.N.L. B, C, D Coy training, A Coy Education	
			Draft of 7 Officers & 962 ORs active from 1/6th Cheshire	

Army Form C. 2118.

Sheet II

WAR DIARY
or
INTELLIGENCE SUMMARY.

(Erase heading not required.)

Instructions regarding War Diaries and Intelligence Summaries are contained in F. S. Regs., Part II. and the Staff Manual respectively. Title pages will be prepared in manuscript.

Place	Date	Hour	Summary of Events and Information	Remarks and references to Appendices
	11/3/19	09.30	Bn paraded for Route march.	Ky.
		17.30	Draft from 1/6th Cheshires inspected by C.O.	Ky.
	12/3/19	09.30	A & B Coy Training. 'C' & 'D' Coy Educational.	Ky.
	13/3/19	09.30	'A', 'C', 'D' Coy Training. 'B' Coy Educational (cancelled)	Ky.
		11.00	Bn inspected by S.O.C. 1st Division	
			Draft of 20 officers & 300 O.Rs arrive from 7th K.S.L.I.	
	14/3/19	09.00	Bn paraded for bathing by Coys.	Ky.
		11.00	Draft from K.S.L.I. inspected by C.O.	Ky.
	15/3/19	09.30	Bn Drill under C.O.	Ky.
	16/3/19	10.40	Bn parade for Divine Service in Cinema Hall.	Ky.
			Major J Richards assumes command of 'C' Coy vice Capt Kennedy.	Lyttyn.
			Capt Pendlebury Arm. do 'B'	Idworth
			Capt Johns dw. do 'D'	
	17/3/19	09.30	'C' & 'D' Coy Training. A' 'B' Coy Education	Ky.
	18/3/19	09.30	Bn parade for Route march.	Ky.
	19/3/19		A & B Coy Training 'C' 'D' Education	Ky.

Army Form C. 2118.

Sheet II

WAR DIARY
or
INTELLIGENCE SUMMARY.
(Erase heading not required.)

Instructions regarding War Diaries and Intelligence Summaries are contained in F.S. Regs., Part II. and the Staff Manual respectively. Title pages will be prepared in manuscript.

Place	Date	Hour	Summary of Events and Information	Remarks and references to Appendices
	11/3/19	0920	Bn paraded for Route march.	Ly.
		17.30	Draft from 1/6th Cheshire inspected by C.O.	Ly.
	12/3/19	0930	A & B Coy training. C & D Coy Educational.	Ly.
	13/3/19	0930	A, C, D Coy training. B Coy Educational (cancelled)	Ly.
		1100	Bn inspected by G.O.C. 1st Division	
			Draft of 20 officers & 300 ORs arrive from 7th I.S.L.I.	Ly.
	14/3/19	0900	Bn paraded for bathing by Coys.	
		1100	Draft from I.S.L.I. inspected by C.O.	Ly.
	15/3/19	0920	Bn Drill under C.O.	Ly.
	16/3/19	1040	Bn parade for Divine service in Cinema Hall.	Ly.
			Major J. Richards assumes command of C Coy vice Capt Kennedy.	
			Capt Pendlebury Hm. do B	Sydgoe
			Capt Johns d/w. do D	Colcastle
	17/3/19	0930	C & D Coy training. A & B Coy Education	Ly.
	18/3/19	0930	Bn parade for Route march	Ly.
	19/3/19		A & B Coy Training. C & D Education	Ly.

Army Form C. 2118.

Instructions regarding War Diaries and Intelligence Summaries are contained in F. S. Regs., Part II. and the Staff Manual respectively. Title pages will be prepared in manuscript.

WAR DIARY
or
INTELLIGENCE SUMMARY.
(Erase heading not required.)

Sheet III.

Place	Date	Hour	Summary of Events and Information	Remarks and references to Appendices
	20/3/19	0930	A',C',D' Coy Training. 'B' Coy Educational Training	
	21/3/19	0900	Bn. parade for talks by Coys.	
	22/3/19	0930	Bn. Drill under C.O.	
	23/3/19	1040	Bn. paraded for Divine Service in Cinema.	
	24/3/19	0930	B', C', D', Coy Training. 'A' Coy Educational Training	
	25/3/19	0930	'A', 'B', Coy Training. 'C', 'D', by Educational Training	
	26/3/19	1000	'A', 'D' turned out on paper chase. 'B', 'C', Coy Education	
		0930	'B' Coy Training.	
	27/3/19	0930	'A' + 'D' Coy Training	
		10-0	'B', 'C' Paper chase.	
	28/3/19	0900	Bn. paraded for bathing by Coys. Coy 1/4 Bn. The Cheshire Regt.	
	29/3/19	0930	Training.	
		11.30 -12.30	Educational Training	
	30/3/19	1040	Bn. paraded for Divine Service in Cinema Hall, Bevenham	
	31/3/19	0930	C' Coy Educational Training A', B', D. Coy Training	
		12.30		

WAR DIARY

or

INTELLIGENCE SUMMARY.

(Erase heading not required.)

Army Form C. 2118.

of 2nd East(ern) L.T.M.B. from 1/7/19 to 31/7/19

Place	Date	Hour	Summary of Events and Information	Remarks and references to Appendices
WEINGARTSGASSE	1/7/19	10.00	Battery moved from WEINGARTSGASSE to P.O.W. Camp WAHN.	
do	29/6/19		LIEUT L.G. BUTLER M.C. assumed temporary command of Battery during the absence of CAPT G.S. DEXTER granted leave 28.6.19 to 12.7.19.	
WAHN	15/7/19	10.00	D.I.O.C. 2nd Eastern Inf. Bde inspected Battery and the various methods of packing guns and ammunition on limber wagons were discussed. Battery fired 15 bomb practice on fire Range at DAVIDSBUSCH.	
WAHN	16/7/19	08.30	Brigade Tactical Exercise. Brigade as Advanced Guard to a Division bringing out the tactical employment of Stokes Guns in the attack.	
WAHN	18/7/19	09.00	Continuation of Brigade Tactical Exercise. Battery represented Enemy troops	
WAHN	29/7/19	09.00		
WAHN	29/7/19	11.00		

www.ingramcontent.com/pod-product-compliance
Lightning Source LLC
Chambersburg PA
CBHW081245170426
43191CB00037B/2047